C000224506

THE WORLD'S BEST
STREET FOOD
RECIPES

igloobooks

Published in 2015
by Igloo Books Ltd
Cottage Farm
Sywell
NN6 0BJ
www.igloobooks.com

Copyright © 2014 Igloo Books Ltd

All rights reserved. No part of this publication may be
reproduced or transmitted in any form or by any means,
electronic, or mechanical, including photocopying, recording,
or by any information storage and retrieval system,
without permission in writing from the publisher.
The measurements used are approximate.

Cover images: Front Ed Freeman / Getty; all additional images Thinkstock / Getty
Endpapers: Front (l) Steven Allen / Getty, (r) Gary Yeowell / Getty;
Back (l) Thinkstock / Getty, (r) Ed Norton / Getty
HUN001 0215
2 4 6 8 10 9 7 5 3 1
ISBN 978-1-78440-304-1

Printed and manufactured in China

CONTENTS

WHAT IS STREET FOOD?

All over the world, exquisite food is being cooked and served up on the street. Out of shacks, on carts, in trucks and vans; the street has become our dining table – and it's wonderful. When you think of street food, you may think of greasy burgers and fried onions, late-night kebabs or soggy chips. But there's more on offer now than ever before. From the South African dish 'Bunny Chow' – a hollowed-out bread loaf filled with curry – to a classic American Philly Cheesesteak, street food is everywhere.

From Europe to Asia, Africa to the Americas, local cuisine is at the heart of the street food culture. These culinary gems are best found on the streets, offering an authentic food sensation that you won't find in any restaurant. It's exciting, exotic and an integral part of culture. And that's why it's so good. Street food is about genuinely great-tasting, artisan cuisine, cooked by professionals who specialise in their chosen dishes.

But you needn't travel the world to get a taste of its finest cuisines. Street food has become stylish and popular, and mobile, pop-up stalls are offering all kinds of cuisines in one place. The options are ever-increasing with the constant flow of culinary trends, with fresher, locally-sourced ingredients being the foundation for some superb menus. There's a revolution taking place on the streets and it's bringing good, real food for everyone, everywhere.

Street food isn't just about the taste; it's also about the experience. It's about eating among the hustle and bustle of life, the passers-by and the fellow diners, surrounded by the enticing aromas of freshly-cooked food and not paying the high prices of Michelin-starred restaurants. It's about an ever-changing menu, seasonal and local ingredients, and the prospect of trying something new without spending a fortune. It's on-the-go, fast food like you've never tasted before.

DISCOVERING STREET FOOD

Although the name says it all, it goes without saying that you may not have a street full of exotic food vendors right on your doorstep. Trendy food stalls often pop up in towns and cities, where the commuters pass through in throngs and hungry tourists flock to delicious smells. In some countries, stalls and shacks are found around every corner or in every hole in the wall, for locals to peruse daily.

If you're looking for something different more locally, why not check out music festivals, arts events or food festivals? These kinds of events are thriving with mobile food vendors, all vying to feed the public food that they are passionate about. Food festivals are ideal for trying new things, and people love to talk about what they're cooking and how they learnt their trade. The sense of community at these events is what brings vendors and buyers back again and again.

Look out for markets, too – vendors flock to give shoppers a taste of something different. This is often where you can find exotic meats or foreign cuisines, as well as the staple street foods you might expect. You can also book many pop-up vendors for your own parties or events – most operate on wheels after all!

ABOUT THIS BOOK

This book is dedicated to street food fanatics who want to recreate mouth-watering dishes in their own home. And for those who haven't yet ventured onto the streets, it's a place to discover new foods. It transports cooks across the globe for a culinary journey, stopping off at the world's most famous street food locations and testing their fast-food delights.

Taking the most popular street food dishes from Europe, the Middle East, Africa, Asia and the Americas, these authentic recipes have been designed with the home cook in mind. Each chapter focuses on a different continent, grouping recipes by country so that you can easily navigate your way through these street food staples; from paella to pizza, currywurst to kofta, baklava to biryani.

If you're struggling to find any ingredients in your local supermarket, have a look in specialist shops or look online. Using, fresh, authentic ingredients will give you the best results.

Burek

Catching up

EUROPE

Paella

On the go

Cornish Pasty

Serves: 4   Preparation time: 30–35 minutes   Cooking time: 25–30 minutes

INGREDIENTS

2 tbsp unsalted butter

1 large onion, finely chopped

2 small white potatoes, peeled and finely diced

½ turnip, peeled and finely diced

450 g / 1 lb / 3 cups steak mince

150 ml / 5 fl. oz / ⅔ cup beef stock

a few dashes of Worcestershire sauce

salt and freshly ground black pepper

250 g / 12 oz / ¾ cup ready-made shortcrust
    pastry

a little plain (all-purpose) flour, for dusting

1 large egg, beaten

1 tbsp whole milk

METHOD

- Melt the butter in a large casserole dish set over a medium heat until hot.

- Add the onion, potato and turnip and sweat for 8–10 minutes, stirring occasionally, until softened.

- Add the steak mince and cook for 4–5 minutes until browned.

- Cover with the stock and Worcestershire sauce, stir well and simmer for 8–10 minutes until most of the liquid has evaporated, then season to taste.

- Preheat the oven to 180°C (160°C fan) / 350F / gas 4.

- Roll out the pastry on a lightly floured surface to 5mm (¼ in) thickness and cut out 10–12 cm (4–5 in) rounds using a straight-sided cookie cutter.

- Fill the centre of the rounds with the beef filling, then wet the edges of the pastry with a little water.

- Fold the pastry over the filling to make half-moon shapes, sealing the pastry using the tines of a fork; arrange on a large baking tray.

- Whisk together the beaten egg and milk and brush over the pasties.

- Bake for 25–30 minutes until golden brown and cooked through.

- Remove to a wire rack to cool before serving warm or cold.

TOP TIP

- For a vegetarian version, try equal measures of turnip, potato, spinach and Cheddar or Gruyère.

13

Crêpes

Serves: 4   Preparation time: 10–15 minutes   Cooking time: 25 minutes

INGREDIENTS

125 g / 4 ½ oz / ¾ cup plain
   (all-purpose) flour

salt and freshly ground black pepper

5 medium eggs

3 tbsp unsalted butter, melted

250 ml / 9 fl. oz / 1 cup semi-skimmed milk

1 tbsp olive oil

100 g / 3 ½ oz / 2 cups baby spinach

METHOD

- Combine the flour and 1 tsp of salt in a large mixing bowl.

- Crack in 1 egg, then whisk, gradually adding the milk, until you have
  a smooth batter, then stir through 1 tbsp of melted butter.

- Heat a little melted butter in a large crêpe pan set over a moderate heat until hot.

- Add a ladle of the crêpe batter and tilt to coat the base of the pan. Once the top
  starts to blister, carefully flip the crêpe and cook the other side for 1 minute.

- Repeat this method, using a little melted butter each time, until you have 4 large
  crêpe, then set to one side and keep warm.

- Cook the remaining eggs in a saucepan of boiling water for 12 minutes, then drain
  and refresh in iced water until cold before peeling and slicing.

- Heat the olive oil in a large frying or sauté pan set over a moderate heat until hot.

- Add the spinach and sauté with a little seasoning until wilted, then drain on
  kitchen paper.

- Spoon the spinach onto the centre of the crêpe and top with sliced eggs, then fold
  the edges in and over the egg; serve immediately.

TOP TIPS

- Thin slices of ham and grated cheese would go perfectly inside these crêpes.

- Asparagus and softly scrambled egg would also make a good alternative; for an
  added luxury, consider stirring some smoked salmon trimmings into the
  scrambled egg.

Waffles

Serves: **4**   Preparation time: **50 minutes**   Cooking time: **12–14 minutes**

INGREDIENTS

300 g / 10 ½ oz / 2 cups plain (all-purpose) flour

1 tsp baking powder

a pinch of salt

2 large eggs

350 ml / 12 oz / 1 ½ cups whole milk, warmed

75 g / 3 oz / ⅓ cup unsalted butter, melted

1 tbsp icing (confectioners') sugar, for dusting

METHOD

- To prepare the batter, combine the flour, baking powder, salt and eggs in a large mixing bowl, whisking well.

- Add the milk in a slow stream, whisking constantly until smooth.

- Add the melted butter and stir a few times, then transfer to a jug and let it stand at room temperature for 30 minutes.

- Once the batter has stood for 25 minutes, preheat a waffle iron according to the manufacturer's instructions.

- Pour the batter into the iron and cook according to the instructions until the waffles are set and golden brown.

- Repeat for each serving and serve warm with a dusting of icing sugar.

TOP TIP

- Try serving these waffles with a generous dollop of dulce de leche on top.

- Melted chocolate and sliced banana make for a delicious, decadent topping.

- A drizzle of warm honey and a sprinkling of chopped nuts would give a nice contrast in textures.

Paella

Serves: **4**   Preparation time: **15 minutes**   Cooking time: **35 minutes**

INGREDIENTS

55 ml / 2 fl. oz / ¼ cup olive oil

1 onion, finely sliced

2 cloves of garlic, finely chopped

1 stalk of celery, finely chopped

1 red pepper, deseeded and sliced

300 g / 10 ½ oz / 1 ½ cups paella rice

a pinch of saffron threads

1.25 l / 2 pints 4 fl. oz / 5 cups hot chicken stock

1 tsp smoked paprika

300 g / 10 ½ oz / 2 cups mussels,
  cleaned with beards removed

2 frozen squid tubes, thawed and sliced into rings

12 raw prawns (shrimp), peeled and de-veined

1 lemon, juiced

salt and freshly ground black pepper

a small bunch of flat-leaf parsley, finely chopped

METHOD

- Heat the olive oil in a large shallow paella dish set over a medium heat until hot. Sweat the onion, garlic and celery for 5–6 minutes until softened and starting to brown.

- Add the pepper and cook for a further 5 minutes, then stir in the paella rice and coat thoroughly in the oil.

- Stir the saffron into the stock, then pour it over the rice.

- Add the paprika, stir well and bring to a simmer, then leave uncovered for 20 minutes.

- Add the seafood and stir well.

- Cook for a further 8–10 minutes, covered, until everything is just cooked through and the mussels have opened; discard any that don't open.

- Stir through the lemon juice and adjust the seasoning to taste.

- Serve in bowls, garnished with chopped parsley.

TOP TIP

- For a meaty version of this paella, try using diced chicken thighs and cubes of chorizo instead of the seafood.

Churros with Thick Hot Chocolate

Serves: **4**   Preparation time: **25 minutes**   Cooking time: **15–20 minutes**

INGREDIENTS

100 g / 3 ½ oz / ⅔ cup plain (all-purpose) flour

100 g / 3 ½ oz / ⅔ cup self-raising flour

a pinch of salt

1 tsp ground cinnamon

110 g / 4 oz / ½ cup caster (superfine) sugar, plus extra for dusting

2 tbsp cornflour (cornstarch)

450 ml / 16 fl. oz / 2 cups boiling water

2 tbsp olive oil

175 ml / 6 fl. oz / ¾ cup whole milk

125 ml / 4 ½ fl. oz / ½ cup double (heavy) cream

150 g / 5 oz / 1 cup good-quality dark chocolate, chopped

150 g / 5 oz / 1 cup good-quality milk chocolate, chopped

1 tbsp golden syrup

1 l / 1 pint 16 fl. oz / 4 cups sunflower oil

METHOD

- Sift together the flours, salt, ground cinnamon, sugar and cornflour into a large mixing bowl.

- Add the boiling water and olive oil, mixing well until you have a soft, sticky dough, adding more water if necessary. Leave to rest for 10 minutes.

- Combine the milk and cream in a large saucepan and heat over a medium heat until boiling.

- Remove from the heat and stir through both chocolates and golden syrup until smooth and thick.

- Heat the oil in a large, heavy-based saucepan to 180°C / 350F.

- Spoon the dough into a large piping bag fitted with a star-shaped nozzle and squeeze into the hot oil, using a pair of scissors to cut the dough at 10 cm (4 in) lengths.

- Cook 2–3 at a time, frying for 3–4 minutes until golden brown.

- Remove from the oil and drain on kitchen paper, dusting immediately with caster sugar.

- Ladle the hot chocolate into serving glasses and serve with the churros on the side.

TOP TIP

- Add a pinch of chilli (chili) powder to the hot chocolate for a Mexican-style kick.

Mini Pizzas

Serves: 8   Preparation time: 1 hour 20–25 minutes   Cooking time: 14–16 minutes

INGREDIENTS

2 tsp caster (superfine) sugar

1 tbsp dried active yeast

150 ml / 5 fl. oz / ⅔ cup warm water

600 g / 1 lb 5 oz / 4 cups strong white bread
   flour, plus extra for kneading

1 tsp salt

2 tbsp extra virgin olive oil

400 g / 14 oz / 2 cups passata

2 tbsp sun-dried tomatoes in oil, drained
   and chopped

300 g / 10 ½ oz / 2 cups canned white crab
   meat, picked through for bone

100 g / 3 ½ oz / 2 cups rocket (arugula)

100 g / 3 ½ oz / 1 cup Parmesan, shaved

salt and freshly ground black pepper

METHOD

- Combine the sugar, yeast and water in a jug; stir once and leave to sit for
  10 minutes until creamy and frothy.

- Place the flour and salt in a large bowl and add the yeast mixture and the oil.
  Mix well until a rough dough starts to form, adding a little more warm water to
  moisten it as necessary.

- Turn out the dough onto a lightly floured surface and knead for 2 minutes.

- Place the dough in a lightly oiled clean bowl and cover with a damp cloth; leave to
  rest for 1 hour in a warm place or until doubled in size.

- Preheat the oven to 220°C (200°C fan) / 425F / gas 7 and place 2 large baking
  trays in the oven to preheat.

- Turn the dough out onto a floured surface and knead briefly, then divide into
  8 equal pieces.

- Roll into small rounds and transfer to the preheated trays.

- Spread the bases with passata, then dot with sun-dried tomatoes and
  crab meat.

- Bake, in 2 batches, for 7–8 minutes, until the base of the dough is cooked
  through and golden.

- Remove from the oven, top with rocket and Parmesan and season to taste
  before serving.

TOP TIP

- These pizzas can be topped with all manner of ingredients; how about fig,
  Gorgonzola and fresh mozzarella?

Arancini

Serves: 8   Preparation time: **30 minutes**   Cooking time: **30 minutes**

INGREDIENTS

55 ml / 2 fl. oz / ¼ cup olive oil

250 g / 9 oz / 1 ⅔ cups vine tomatoes, cored, deseeded and diced

salt and freshly ground black pepper

300 g / 10 ½ oz / 2 ½ cups Arborio rice

1 l / 1 pint 16 fl. oz / 4 cups hot vegetable stock

100 g / 3 ½ oz / 1 cup mozzarella, cubed

55 g / 2 oz / ½ cup Parmesan, grated

2 tbsp basil leaves, finely sliced

2 medium eggs, beaten

225 g / 8 oz / 2 cups golden breadcrumbs

1.5 l / 2 pints 12 fl. oz / 6 cups vegetable oil, for deep-frying

a few sprigs of basil, to garnish

METHOD

- Heat the olive oil in a saucepan set over a moderate heat until hot, then fry the tomatoes for 2–3 minutes until softened.

- Season with salt and pepper and add the rice, stirring well to coat in the oil.

- Cover with the stock and bring to the boil; cook for 10–12 minutes until al dente.

- Meanwhile, in a small mixing bowl, combine the mozzarella cubes with the Parmesan and some black pepper.

- Remove the rice from the heat and stir through the basil before spreading it out on a large baking tray to cool.

- Once the rice is cool enough to handle, oil your hands and shape small handfuls of the rice into 8 balls.

- Place a little of the cheese filling in the middle and close your hand to form a ball around the filling.

- Roll the rice balls in the beaten egg and then gently in the breadcrumbs, making sure they are coated evenly.

- Heat the vegetable oil in a large, heavy-based saucepan to 170°C / 340F.

- Deep-fry the arancini, four at a time, for 6–8 minutes until golden brown and crisp, then drain on kitchen paper.

- Serve the arancini with sprigs of basil.

TOP TIPS

- Other fillings that would work well include diced ham, chopped prawns and shredded bresaola.

- For a vegetarian spin, place a sautéed button mushroom or Chanterelle in the middle.

Gelato

Serves: **4–6**   Preparation time: **4 hours 20–25 minutes**   Cooking time: **15–25 minutes**

INGREDIENTS

4 large egg yolks

150 g / 5 oz / ⅔ cup golden caster
   (superfine) sugar

500 ml / 18 fl. oz / 2 cups whole milk

225 ml / 8 fl. oz / 1 cup double (heavy) cream

1 vanilla pod, split lengthwise

4–6 ice-cream cones

METHOD

- Whisk together the egg yolks and sugar in a large heatproof bowl until pale and thick.
- Heat together the milk, cream and vanilla pod in a saucepan set over a medium heat; remove from the heat once the mixture starts to simmer.
- Scrape the vanilla seeds out of the pod and add them to the milk, then discard the pod.
- Whisk roughly a third of the liquid onto the egg yolk mixture, then add the rest of the mixture in a slow, steady stream, whisking all the time.
- Pour the mixture back into a saucepan and cook over a low heat, stirring frequently, until thickened and of coating consistency.
- Strain the custard into a clean bowl, then chill for 4 hours until cold.
- Churn the cold custard according to the manufacturer's instructions in an ice-cream maker.
- Once the gelato is soft yet frozen, either serve immediately in cones or cover and freeze.

TOP TIPS

- For coffee gelato, add 125 ml / 4 fl. oz / ½ cup of chilled, strong coffee to the custard before churning.
- Add 100 g / 3 ½ oz / ⅔ cup of strawberry or raspberry purée to the chilled custard before churning for berry gelato.

Lamb Souvlaki

Serves: 4   Preparation time: 1 hour 20 minutes   Cooking time: 10–12 minutes

INGREDIENTS

55 ml / 2 fl. oz / ¼ cup olive oil

55 ml / 2 fl. oz / ¼ cup red wine

2 tbsp red wine vinegar

2 tsp dried oregano

2 cloves of garlic, crushed

a pinch of chilli (chili) flakes

salt and freshly ground black pepper

500 g / 1 lb 2 oz / 2 cups lamb neck fillet, trimmed and cubed

150 g / 5 oz / ⅔ cup Greek yoghurt

a small bunch of mint, finely chopped

1 lemon, juiced

4 cherry tomatoes

4 white pitta breads

½ iceberg lettuce, shredded

1 large white onion, sliced

4 large vine tomatoes, cored and chopped

METHOD

- In a large mixing bowl, whisk together the olive oil, red wine, red wine vinegar, oregano, garlic, chilli flakes and seasoning.
- Add the lamb and stir well, then cover and chill for up to 1 hour.
- Preheat a grill or barbecue to a moderately hot temperature.
- Whisk together the Greek yoghurt with half of the mint, a dash of lemon juice and some seasoning, then cover and chill.
- Thread the lamb onto metal skewers with a cherry tomato threaded in the middle of the skewer.
- Grill for 10–12 minutes, turning frequently, until firm yet a little springy to the touch.
- Let the lamb skewers rest for a few minutes before serving in the pitta breads with a dollop of mint yoghurt and some lettuce, onion and tomato.
- Garnish with more chopped mint and a drizzle of lemon juice before serving.

TOP TIP

- The pitta breads can be toasted for 1 minute in a toaster or under a grill to warm them through.

Currywurst

Serves: **4**   Preparation time: **10 minutes**   Cooking time: **30 minutes**

INGREDIENTS

1 tbsp sunflower oil

1 tsp onion powder

1 tsp sweet paprika

1 tbsp curry power (mild or hot), plus extra for garnishing

350 g / 12 oz / 1 ½ cups tomato ketchup

175 ml / 6 fl. oz / ¾ cup cold water

4 medium bratwurst sausages

salt and freshly ground black pepper

METHOD

- Heat the oil in a large saucepan set over a medium heat until hot.

- Add the onion powder, paprika and curry powder, then stir well and cook for 1 minute before covering with the ketchup and water.

- Bring the sauce to the boil, then simmer for approximately 15 minutes until thickened.

- Preheat the grill to hot.

- Grill the bratwurst for 8–10 minutes, turning occasionally, until dark brown and sizzling.

- Remove from the grill and leave to rest for a few minutes.

- Season the sauce to taste and slice the bratwurst and arrange in dishes.

- Top with the curry sauce and a pinch of curry powder before serving.

TOP TIP

- Grate some mild Cheddar over the currywurst before flashing under the grill until bubbling.

Burek

Serves: 4   Preparation time: 25–30 minutes   Cooking time: 20–25 minutes

INGREDIENTS

4 large eggs

450 g / 1 lb / 8 cups baby spinach, washed

2 tbsp olive oil

2 cloves of garlic

2 tsp paprika

a pinch of ground cumin

salt and freshly ground black pepper

150 g / 5 oz / 1 ½ cups Cheddar, grated

4 ready-made filo pastry sheets

55 g / 2 oz / ¼ cup unsalted butter, melted

METHOD

- Cook the eggs in a large saucepan of boiling water for 12 minutes, then drain and refresh in iced water.

- Preheat the oven to 190°C (170°C fan) / 375F / gas 5 and line 2 baking trays with greaseproof paper.

- Bring a large saucepan of salted water to the boil and blanch the spinach for 1 minute.

- Drain and leave to cool, then press the spinach against the sides of a colander to extract as much excess water as you can.

- Chop the spinach and set to one side. Heat the olive oil in a large sauté pan set over a moderate heat until hot.

- Fry the garlic for 1 minute, then add the spinach and continue to cook for 2 minutes before adding the spices and seasoning.

- Tip the spinach into a bowl and season with plenty of salt and pepper.

- Peel the eggs and finely chop, then add them to the spinach along with the cheese and stir well.

- Brush the sheets of filo with a little melted butter, then fold one corner over to the opposite corner so that you have a triangle shape.

- Spoon the filling into the centre of the filo, then bring one of the corners over the filling and seal well against the other corner.

- Place the parcels on the baking tray and brush with more melted butter, then bake for 20–25 minutes until golden and crisp.

- Remove from the oven and leave to cool slightly before serving.

TOP TIP

- For a cheesy version of this dish, replace the eggs and spinach mixture with equal amounts of feta cheese and mozzarella, a bunch of chopped dill and some black pepper.

Khachupuri

Makes: 2   Preparation time: 1 hour 5–10 minutes   Cooking time: 20–23 minutes

INGREDIENTS

1 tsp dried active yeast

a pinch of caster (superfine) sugar

150 ml / 5 fl. oz / ⅔ cup lukewarm water

2 tbsp olive oil

200 g / 7 oz / 1 ⅓ cups plain (all-purpose) flour,
    plus extra for dusting

1 tsp salt

100 g / 3 ½ oz / 1 cup grated Cheddar

100 g / 3 ½ oz / 1 cup grated mozzarella

2 medium eggs

2 tbsp butter, softened

METHOD

- Combine the yeast, sugar and water in a bowl and leave to stand for
  10–15 minutes until foamy.

- Add 1 tbsp of oil, the flour and salt and mix well until a soft dough starts to come
  together.

- Turn out the dough onto a lightly floured surface and knead for 4–5 minutes until
  smooth and elastic.

- Sit the dough in a lightly oiled bowl, cover loosely with a damp tea towel
  and leave to prove in a warm place for approximately 45 minutes until doubled
  in size.

- Preheat the oven to 230°C (210°C fan) / 450F / gas 8.

- Once the dough has doubled in size, turn it out and knock it down with your hands,
  then divide in half.

- Roll the pieces of dough into 25 cm (10 in) rounds and sprinkle half of both
  cheeses onto the rounds, leaving a 1–2 cm (½ –1 in) border.

- Bring the sides of the dough up and over the cheese, pinching the ends together
  and shaping the dough into a canoe shape; leave a hole in the middle.

- Sprinkle the rest of the cheese into the holes and transfer the breads onto a large
  baking tray.

- Brush with the remaining olive oil and bake for 16–18 minutes until golden all
  over, then remove from the oven and carefully crack an egg into the middle of
  each hole.

- Return to the oven for 4–5 minutes until the egg is set, then remove from the
  oven and brush with softened butter before serving.

TOP TIP

- This bread is best eaten hot – tear off the ends and dunk them in the cheese and
  egg mixture in the middle.

Blinis

Serves: 4   Preparation time: 10–15 minutes   Cooking time: 15–20 minutes

INGREDIENTS

200 g / 7 oz / 1 cup plain yoghurt

a small bunch of chives, finely chopped

salt and freshly ground black pepper

55 g / 2 oz / ⅓ cup buckwheat flour

110 g / 4 oz / ⅔ cup strong white bread flour

¾ tsp salt

½ tsp baking powder

1 ½ tsp fast-action dried yeast

150 g / 5 oz / ⅔ cup crème fraiche

175 ml / 6 fl. oz / ¾ cup semi-skimmed milk

2 medium egg yolks

2 tbsp unsalted butter, melted

150 g / 5 oz / 1 cup smoked salmon slices

1 lemon, juiced

METHOD

- Whisk together the yoghurt, chopped chives and seasoning in a small bowl, then cover and chill.

- Prepare the blini batter by sifting together the flours, salt and baking powder into a large mixing bowl.

- Sprinkle the yeast on top, then combine the crème fraiche and milk in a saucepan and heat together very gently. Remove from the heat and whisk in the egg yolks until smooth.

- Pour on top of the flour mixture and whisk until smooth, then set to one side.

- Brush the base of a blini pan or frying pan with a little melted butter and heat over a moderate heat until hot.

- Add small ladles of the batter to the pan and cook the blinis, 3 or 4 at a time, until set and golden underneath. Flip and cook the other side for 1 minute, then transfer to a lined plate.

- Dress the salmon with lemon juice before folding on top of the blinis.

- Serve with the chive yoghurt on top.

TOP TIP

- These blinis can be served with warmed dulce de leche and a sprinkling of chopped nuts or sliced banana on top for a sweet version.

Tabbouleh

Sights and sounds

• MIDDLE EAST & AFRICA •

Bunny Chow

A friendly welcome

Falafel

Makes: 12   Preparation time: 20–25 minutes   Cooking time: 12–15 minutes

INGREDIENTS

3 tbsp sunflower oil

1 onion, finely chopped

2 cloves of garlic, crushed

2 tsp ground cumin

1 tsp ground coriander

600 g / 1 lb 5 oz / 3 cups canned chickpeas
    (garbanzo beans), drained and rinsed

a small bunch of flat-leaf parsley, finely chopped

1 large egg, beaten

100 g / 3 ½ oz / ⅔ cup plain (all-purpose) flour

salt and freshly ground black pepper

METHOD

- Preheat the oven to 200°C (180°C fan) / 400F / gas 6 and line a baking tray with greaseproof paper.

- Heat 1 tbsp of oil in a frying pan over a moderate heat until hot, then sweat the onion and garlic for 4–5 minutes, stirring occasionally, until soft.

- Continue cooking for a further 2–3 minutes until the onion and garlic start to brown, then add the spices and stir well before transferring to a mixing bowl.

- Add the chickpeas and mash using a potato masher until they are broken down.

- Stir in the parsley, the beaten egg and some seasoning and mix well using your hands.

- Take tablespoons of the mixture and mould into small balls using the palms of your hands, then roll the balls in the flour, shaking off any excess.

- Heat the remaining sunflower oil in a large frying pan over a moderate heat and brown the falafels all over.

- Arrange on the baking tray and bake for 12–15 minutes until golden brown and crisp.

- Remove and serve warm or cold.

Tabbouleh

Serves: **4**   Preparation time: **20 minutes**

INGREDIENTS

225 g / 8 oz / 1 cup fine bulgar wheat

100 ml / 3 ½ fl. oz / ½ cup olive oil

250 ml / 9 fl. oz / 1 cup boiling water

2 large vine tomatoes, cored, deseeded and diced

a small bunch of coriander (cilantro), finely chopped

a small bunch of mint, finely chopped

a large bunch of flat-leaf parsley, finely chopped

2 lemons, juiced

salt and freshly ground black pepper

METHOD

- Place the bulgar wheat in a large heatproof bowl.
- Coat with half of the olive oil, then pour over the boiling water and stir briefly.
- Cover the bowl tightly with cling film and let it stand for 10 minutes.
- Drain the bulgar wheat through a fine sieve, pressing on it to remove any excess water.
- Transfer to a large mixing bowl and toss with the tomato and herbs.
- Add the rest of the olive oil and lemon juice and stir thoroughly.
- Season to taste before serving or chilling.

TOP TIP

- Draining any juices from the chopped tomatoes before adding them to the bowl will help to keep the tabbouleh crisp and fresh for longer.

Lamb Kofta and Pitta Bread

Serves: **4**   Preparation time: **15 minutes**   Cooking time: **18–22 minutes**

INGREDIENTS

500 g / 1 lb 2 oz / 3 ⅓ cups lamb mince

1 tsp ground cumin

1 tsp ground coriander

½ tsp dried oregano

a small bunch of mint leaves, picked and
    finely chopped

2 cloves of garlic, minced

salt and freshly ground black pepper

4 large white pitta breads

½ iceberg lettuce, shredded

½ small cucumber, sliced

2 large vine tomatoes, cored and thinly sliced

1 small red onion, finely sliced

½ lemon, juiced

METHOD

- Preheat the oven to 190°C (170°C fan) / 375F / gas 5 and grease and line a large baking tray with greaseproof paper.
- Thoroughly combine the lamb mince, cumin, coriander, oregano, mint, garlic and plenty of seasoning in a large mixing bowl.
- Divide the mixture into 8 and shape into kofta using your hands.
- Arrange the kofta on the prepared baking tray and bake for 18–22 minutes until golden brown all over and sizzling.
- Remove the kofta from the oven when ready and keep warm to one side. Place the pittas in the oven to warm through for 2 minutes.
- Remove the pitta and top with a mixture of the salad ingredients followed by the kofta.
- Drizzle with a little lemon juice and serve immediately.

TOP TIP

- The tabbouleh on the previous page makes a great side salad to go with this dish.

Martabak

Serves: 4   Preparation time: 30–35 minutes   Cooking time: 20–25 minutes

INGREDIENTS

300 g / 10 ½ oz / 2 cups strong white bread flour, plus extra for dusting

1 tsp caster (superfine) sugar

½ tsp salt

½ tsp baking powder

150 ml / 5 fl. oz / ⅔ cup semi-skimmed milk

2 tbsp butter, melted

2 tbsp olive oil

2 cloves of garlic, minced

1 large red pepper, deseeded and finely diced

1 tsp ground cumin

a pinch of ground coriander

a pinch of ground cinnamon

salt and freshly ground black pepper

400 g / 14 oz / 2 cups canned tuna chunks, drained

55 g / 2 oz / ½ cup feta, crumbled

METHOD

- Combine the flour, sugar, salt and baking powder in a large mixing bowl and stir well.

- Whisk together the milk and butter in a jug, then stir into the dry ingredients until a soft dough starts to form.

- Turn out the dough onto a lightly floured surface and knead for 8–10 minutes until smooth and elastic.

- Place the dough in a lightly oiled bowl and cover with a damp cloth; leave to prove in a warm place for 15 minutes.

- Preheat the oven to 190°C (170°C fan) / 375F / gas 5.

- Heat the olive oil in a sauté pan set over a moderate heat until hot.

- Sauté the garlic and pepper for 2 minutes, then add the spices and seasoning.

- Stir well and remove from the heat before adding the tuna and feta; stir thoroughly to combine.

- After the dough has proved, divide it into 8 and shape into balls.

- Roll out the dough on a lightly floured surface into rounds approximately 5 mm (¼) in thick.

- Spoon the tuna filling onto the centre of half of the rounds and wet the rims with a little water.

- Place the remaining rounds on top and seal well, pricking all over with a fork.

- Carefully lift onto baking trays and bake for 20–25 minutes until the dough is golden and cooked.

- Remove from the oven and leave to cool slightly before cutting and serving.

TOP TIP

- Martabak also works well with either cooked lamb or beef mince stuffing instead of tuna.

Stuffed Vine Leaves

Serves: 4   Preparation time: 10–15 minutes   Cooking time: 10 minutes

INGREDIENTS

2 tbsp olive oil

1 onion, finely chopped

2 cloves of garlic, minced

a pinch of cumin seeds

a pinch of ground cinnamon

2 tbsp white wine

250 g / 9 oz / 2 cups cooked long-grain rice

55 g / 2 oz / ⅓ cup raisins

1 Granny Smith apple, cored and finely diced

salt and freshly ground black pepper

8 vine leaves in brine, drained

a few sprigs of mint leaves

2 tbsp extra virgin olive oil

METHOD

- Heat the olive oil in a large sauté pan set over a medium heat until hot.

- Add the onion, garlic and cumin seeds and sauté for 4–5 minutes until softened.

- Add the ground cinnamon and stir well, then add the wine, rice, raisins and apple.

- Cook for 4–5 minutes until the rice is warmed through, then season to taste.

- Spoon the rice onto the centre of the vine leaves, then fold and roll them securely.

- Serve with sprigs of mint and a drizzle of extra virgin olive oil.

TOP TIP

- If you can't find vine leaves, cabbage leaves are a good substitute.

Fattoush

Serves: 4   Preparation time: 10–15 minutes   Cooking time: 10 minutes

INGREDIENTS

55 ml / 2 fl. oz / ¼ cup olive oil

2 white pitta breads, chopped

salt and freshly ground black pepper

75 ml / 3 fl. oz / ⅓ cup extra virgin olive oil

2 tbsp white wine vinegar

a pinch of caster (superfine) sugar

1 clove of garlic, minced

a small handful of radishes, sliced thinly

300 g / 10 ½ oz / 2 cups cherry tomatoes, halved

1 large cucumber, deseeded and finely diced

2 spring onions (scallions), finely sliced

1 red pepper, deseeded and finely diced

a small bunch of mint, finely chopped

a small bunch of flat-leaf parsley, finely chopped

1 lemon, juiced

METHOD

- Heat the olive oil in a large sauté pan set over a moderate heat until hot.

- Add the chopped pitta bread and fry until golden and crisp, then drain on kitchen paper and season with salt.

- Whisk together the extra virgin olive oil, white wine vinegar, sugar, garlic and seasoning in a large mixing bowl.

- Add the radishes, cherry tomatoes, cucumber, spring onion, pepper, chopped herbs and lemon juice.

- Toss well to coat, then add the pitta bread and toss again. Season to taste before serving.

TOP TIP

- Sliced black olives would lend a welcome savoury punch to this salad.

Baklava

Serves: 8   Preparation time: 15–20 minutes   Cooking time: 1–1 ¼ hours

INGREDIENTS

150 g / 5 oz / 1 ½ cups cashews

150 g / 5 oz / 1 ½ cups hazelnuts (cobnuts)

400 g / 14 oz / 2 cups caster (superfine) sugar

75 g / 3 oz / ⅓ cup runny honey

2 tsp ground cinnamon

½ tsp ground cloves

350 g / 12 oz / 1 ½ cups unsalted butter, melted

14 ready-made large filo pastry sheets,
      kept under a damp cloth

250 ml / 9 fl. oz / 1 cup water

METHOD

- Preheat the oven to 170°C (150°C fan) / 325°F / gas 3.

- Blitz the nuts in a food processor until finely chopped and tip into a mixing bowl.

- Add 55 g / 2 oz / ¼ cup of sugar and honey, 1 tsp of ground cinnamon and the ground cloves and stir well.

- Brush a large non-stick roasting tray with some of the melted butter.

- Cut a pastry sheet to size and cover the base of the tray with it.

- Brush the top of the pastry with more melted butter.

- Repeat this process until you have a stack of 6 buttered sheets of filo pastry.

- Sprinkle the filling mixture on top and smooth it level with the back of a wet tablespoon.

- Brush the top with melted butter, then repeat the layering process until you have a stack of 10 sheets of filo pastry with melted butter in between each layer.

- Bake for 1–1 ¼ hours until golden all over on top.

- Meanwhile, combine the remaining sugar, honey and cinnamon with the water in a large saucepan.

- Bring to boiling point over a moderate heat, then reduce to a simmer for 10 minutes until syrupy.

- Set to one side to cool while the baklava finishes baking in the oven.

- Remove the baklava when ready and allow it to sit for a minute, then pour the syrup over the top.

- Allow to cool before cutting into pieces and serving.

TOP TIP

- These super-sweet treats are perfect served with a small cup of strong coffee.

Koshari

Serves: 4   Preparation time: 15–20 minutes   Cooking time: 35 minutes

INGREDIENTS

225 g / 8 oz / 2 cups spaghetti

165 g / 5 ½ oz / 1 ½ cups ditalini

150 g / 5 oz / ⅔ cup green lentils

55 ml / 2 fl. oz / ¼ cup sunflower oil

2 large onions, thinly sliced

1 tbsp ground cumin

2 tsp ground black peppercorns

2 tsp paprika

2 tsp ground coriander

½ tsp ground cloves

½ tsp ground cardamom

400 g / 14 oz / 2 cups canned chickpeas
    (garbanzo beans), drained

125 g / 4 ½ oz / 1 cup cooked basmati rice

salt and freshly ground black pepper

METHOD

- Cook the spaghetti and ditalini in a large saucepan of salted, boiling water for 8–10 minutes until al dente.

- Drain the cooking liquid into another saucepan and return it to the boil. Set the pasta to one side.

- Add the lentils to the cooking liquid and cook for 10–12 minutes until tender, then drain and leave to cool slightly.

- Heat the oil in a large sauté pan set over a moderate heat until hot.

- Add the onions and some salt; fry until golden and crisp, then remove from the pan and draining on kitchen paper.

- Add the ground spices to the oil in the pan and fry for 1 minute, then add the chickpeas and rice.

- Sauté over a reduced heat for 3–4 minutes, then add the cooked pasta and lentils.

- Toss everything well with a pair of tongs, then season to taste and lift into bowls.

- Serve with the onions on top.

TOP TIP

- If you can't find ditalini, macaroni will work just as well.

Halva

Serves: 6-8   Preparation time: 15 minutes + 36 hours chilling   Cooking time: 15 minutes

INGREDIENTS

450 g / 1 lb / 2 cups honey

375 g / 13 oz / 1 ½ cups tahini

150 g / 5 oz / 1 ½ cups shelled pistachios

METHOD

- Place the honey in a heavy-based saucepan set over a medium heat and cook until it reaches 115°C / 240F on a sugar or instant-read thermometer.

- Set the honey to one side and heat the tahini in a separate saucepan until it reads 50°C / 122F on the thermometer.

- Add the tahini to the honey and stir thoroughly until smooth and even.

- Stir in the pistachios and continue to stir for 5–7 minutes until the mixture starts to stiffen.

- Pour the mixture into a greased and lined baking tin. Let it cool to room temperature, then wrap it in cling film and chill for at least 36 hours.

- Remove the halva after 36 hours and let it warm to room temperature before serving.

TOP TIP

- There are many variations on halva – for an alternative taste, try replacing the pistachios with almonds, sunflower seeds, peanuts or raisins.

Biryani

Serves: **4**   Preparation time: **20 minutes**   Cooking time: **30 minutes**

INGREDIENTS

2 large onions, roughly chopped

4 cloves of garlic, minced

5 cm (2 in) piece of root ginger, peeled

2 red chillies (chilies), deseeded and chopped

75 ml / 3 fl. oz / ⅓ cup sunflower oil

500 g / 1 lb 2 oz piece of boneless lamb
shoulder, diced

1 tbsp ground cumin

1 tsp ground coriander

2 tsp garam masala

2 tsp ground turmeric

1 tsp Madras curry powder

salt and freshly ground pepper

300g / 11 oz / 1 ½ cups basmati rice, soaked in
warm water for 15 minutes, then rinsed with
cold water several times

875 ml / 1 pint 10 fl. oz / 3 ½ cups lamb stock

1 lemon, juiced

2 tbsp cashews

a small handful of coriander (cilantro),
leaves picked

METHOD

- Place the onions, garlic, ginger and chillies in a food processor and pulse with a little water until you have a smooth purée.

- Heat the sunflower oil in a large casserole dish over a moderate heat until hot.

- Fry the onion purée for 4–5 minutes, stirring occasionally until light brown, then sprinkle over the ground spices and some salt and pepper.

- Add the diced lamb to the pan and cook, stirring frequently, for 5–6 minutes until aromatic and lightly sealed.

- Stir in the rinsed rice, then cover with the stock.

- Cover with a tight-fitting lid and bring to a vigorous, rolling boil, then lower to a gentle simmer for 15–20 minutes until the rice has absorbed the stock.

- Remove from the heat and set to one side for 15 minutes, still covered.

- Season to taste with lemon juice, salt and pepper, before serving in bowls garnished with cashews and coriander leaves.

TOP TIP

- A small handful of pomegranate seeds or raisins can be stirred into the biryani before serving.

Bunny Chow

Serves: 4   Preparation time: 15–20 minutes   Cooking time: 35–45 minutes

INGREDIENTS

55 ml / 2 fl. oz / ¼ cup vegetable oil

2 small onions, finely chopped

3 cloves of garlic, minced

5 cm (2 in) piece of root ginger, minced

2 large carrots, peeled and chopped

2 tsp ground cumin

2 tsp ground coriander

2 tsp Madras curry powder

a pinch of Cayenne pepper

600 g / 1 lb 5 oz lamb neck fillet, cut into chunks

125 ml / 4 ½ fl. oz / ½ cup water

1 tbsp tomato purée

a pinch of caster (superfine) sugar

400 g / 14 oz / 2 cups passata

250 ml / 9 fl. oz / 1 cup lamb stock

salt and freshly ground black pepper

1 large French boule loaf

a few sprigs of flat-leaf parsley, to garnish

METHOD

- Heat the vegetable oil in a large saucepan set over a medium heat until hot.

- Sauté the onion, garlic, ginger and carrots for 3–4 minutes until lightly browned.

- Add the ground spices, stir briefly and continue to cook for 1 minute.

- Add the lamb and brown well, then add the water, tomato purée and sugar.

- Stir well before adding the passata and lamb stock, then stir again.

- Reduce the heat to low and cook, uncovered, for 35–45 minutes until the lamb is tender.

- Once tender, remove the lamb from the sauce and set to one side.

- Blitz the sauce in a food processor until smooth, then adjust the seasoning to taste.

- Use a bread knife to cut out a round from the top of the boule. Use your hands to hollow out the rest of the boule.

- Fill the boule with the curry sauce and lamb; garnish with cubes of the hollowed-out bread and a sprig of parsley.

TOP TIP

- Spoon over a little crème fraiche or sour cream for a cooling counterpoint to the curry.

Samosas

A feast for the senses

· ASIA ·

Bibimbap

Freshly made

Satay Chicken

Serves: 4   Preparation time: 15 minutes   Cooking time: 15 minutes

INGREDIENTS

225g / 8 oz / 1 cup smooth peanut butter

110 ml / 4 fl. oz / ½ cup warm water

2 tbsp light soy sauce

2 tbsp lime juice

4 small skinless chicken breasts, cut into strips

a few sprigs of coriander (cilantro), to garnish

METHOD

- Soak 8 wooden skewers in cold water for 30 minutes.
- Meanwhile, whisk together the peanut butter, water, soy sauce and lime juice in a small saucepan until smooth.
- Cook over a medium heat for 2–3 minutes, stirring frequently, until simmering.
- Remove from the heat and leave to cool for 5 minutes. Preheat the grill to hot.
- Thread the strips of chicken onto the skewers and brush with the satay sauce.
- Arrange on a grilling tray and grill for 6–8 minutes, turning once, until golden and cooked through.
- Remove from the grill and leave to cool for a few minutes, then serve with sprigs of coriander.

TOP TIP

- If you like your satay with a bit of a kick, add 1 tsp chilli (chili) powder to the peanut butter sauce or serve the chicken skewers with some sweet chilli sauce.

Nasi Goreng

Serves: 4   Preparation time: 10–15 minutes   Cooking time: 15 minutes

INGREDIENTS

2 tbsp fish sauce

1 tbsp dark brown soft sugar

2 limes, juiced

2 tbsp warm water

55 ml / 2 fl. oz / ¼ cup groundnut oil

salt and freshly ground black pepper

2 large skinless chicken breasts, sliced

350 g / 12 oz / 2 ⅓ cups raw prawns (shrimp),
    peeled and de-veined

2 shallots, finely chopped

2 cloves of garlic, minced

3 cm (1 in) piece of root ginger, peeled
    and grated

2 tsp curry powder

1 tsp ground turmeric

½ tsp ground nutmeg

350 g / 12 oz / 3 cups cooked brown
    basmati rice

2 spring onions (scallions), green tops
    finely sliced

2 red chillies (chilies), sliced

METHOD

- Whisk together the fish sauce, sugar, lime juice and water in a small bowl, then set to one side.
- Heat 2 tbsp of the oil in a large wok set over a moderate heat until hot.
- Season the chicken before stir-frying for 4–5 minutes, then transfer to a plate.
- Add another tablespoon of oil to the wok and season the prawns before stir-frying for 2 minutes until pink.
- Remove the prawns from the wok and reduce the heat under the wok a little.
- Add the rest of the oil and sauté the shallots, garlic and ginger for 2–3 minutes, then add the ground spices.
- Stir well and cook for 1 minute, then add the chicken back to the wok.
- Stir well, then add the rice. Continue to cook for 4–5 minutes until the rice is warmed through.
- Add the prawns and stir well, then add the prepared sauce. Stir well again and cook for a few more minutes until the sauce has reduced slightly.
- Season to taste before spooning onto plates and garnishing with the sliced spring onion and chilli.

TOP TIP

- Stir 2 eggs into the wok at the same time as the rice and allow them to cook through to vary the taste and texture of this dish.

Wonton Soup

Serves: 4   Preparation time: 35–40 minutes   Cooking time: 8–10 minutes

INGREDIENTS

300 g / 10 ½ oz / 2 cups raw prawns, peeled, de-veined and chopped

200 g / 7 oz / 1 ⅓ cups pork mince

2 tbsp light soy sauce

2 tbsp rice wine

2 tbsp sesame oil

1 tsp caster (superfine) sugar

a pinch of red chilli (chili) flakes

2 spring onions (scallions), finely chopped

1 small egg white, lightly beaten

salt and freshly ground black pepper

250 g / 9 oz ready-made wonton wrappers

1.25 l / 2 pints 4 fl. oz / 5 cups chicken stock

½ small Chinese cabbage, leaves separated and roughly chopped

METHOD

- Thoroughly mix the prawns, pork mince and 1 tbsp each of the soy sauce, rice wine and sesame oil with the sugar, chilli flakes, spring onions, egg white and seasoning in a large mixing bowl.

- Cover the bowl and chill for 15 minutes.

- Fill the wontons by placing a small tablespoon of the filling in the centre of the wrappers, then wet the rim with a little water and bring the edges up and around the filling.

- Pinch together the edges at the top to seal well, then repeat with the other wontons.

- Combine the chicken stock with the remaining soy sauce, rice wine and sesame oil in a saucepan.

- Bring to a simmer over a medium heat before adding the Chinese cabbage. Bring a large saucepan of salted water to the boil.

- Poach the wontons, in batches if necessary, in the salted water for 1 minute or until they float to the surface of the water.

- Transfer the poached wontons to the chicken broth and cook over a reduced heat for 2 minutes.

- Adjust the seasoning of the broth to taste, then ladle the soup into bowls and serve.

TOP TIP

- These wontons also work well steamed or deep-fried and served with a sweet chilli sauce for dipping.

Spring Rolls

Makes: **8**   Preparation time: **30 minutes**   Cooking time: **6 minutes**

INGREDIENTS

a small bunch of coriander (cilantro)

4 large spring onions (scallions), sliced thinly
lengthways

2 carrots, peeled and julienned

2 tbsp rice wine vinegar

1 tbsp oyster sauce

1 tbsp dark soy sauce

2 tsp Chinese five-spice

300 g / 10 ½ oz / 2 cups white crab meat, picked
through for bone

8 Chinese spring roll wrappers, covered with a
damp cloth

1 egg yolk, beaten

1.25 l / 2 pints 4 fl. oz / 5 cups groundnut oil

1 lemon, cut into wedges

METHOD

- Finely chop most of the coriander; retain a few sprigs for a garnish.

- In a mixing bowl, combine the spring onions, carrots, chopped coriander, rice
wine vinegar, oyster sauce, soy sauce, five-spice and crab meat and toss well.

- Lay a spring roll wrapper on a flat surface and brush the edges with a little
egg yolk.

- Spoon a few tablespoons of the filling into the lower section of the spring rolls
and fold the edges inwards to just cover the filling.

- Bring the bottom edge of the wrapper over the filling and begin to carefully roll
until you have the shape of a spring roll.

- Repeat the process for the rest of the spring rolls; cover with a damp cloth to
prevent the completed ones from drying out.

- Heat the groundnut oil in a large, heavy-based saucepan to 180°C / 350F.

- Carefully lower 4 spring rolls at a time into the hot oil and deep-fry for
3 minutes until golden brown.

- Remove and drain on kitchen paper before serving with lemon wedges and
coriander sprigs.

TOP TIP

- Shredded chicken or duck both make an excellent meaty alternative to seafood.

- For vegetarian fillings, try using sliced tofu or chopped, mixed wild mushrooms.

Samosas

Serves: 8   Preparation time: **30 minutes**   Cooking time: **8–10 minutes**

INGREDIENTS

½ small cucumber

250 g / 9 oz / 1 cup plain yoghurt

salt and freshly ground black pepper

55 ml / 2 fl. oz / ¼ cup sunflower oil

2 onions, finely chopped

2 cloves of garlic, minced

5 cm (2 in) piece of root ginger,
    peeled and minced

2 tsp ground cumin

2 tsp ground coriander

1 tsp mild curry powder

½ tsp garam masala

½ tsp paprika

a pinch of caster (superfine) sugar

450 g / 1 lb / 3 cups floury potatoes, peeled
    and finely diced

150 g / 5 oz / 3 cups baby spinach, washed

1.25 l / 2 pints 4 fl. oz / 5 cups vegetable oil,
    for deep-frying

8 samosa wrappers

a few sprigs of mint, to garnish

METHOD

- Grate the cucumber and press through a sieve to extract as much water
  as possible.

- Place in a mixing bowl and stir in the yoghurt. Season to taste before covering
  and chilling.

- Meanwhile, heat the sunflower oil in a large saucepan set over a medium heat.

- Sweat the onion, garlic and ginger for 6–7 minutes, stirring occasionally, then
  add the ground spices, sugar and seasoning. Stir well.

- Add the potato and stir well, then cover with a lid and reduce the heat
  a little.

- Once the potato is softened, remove the lid and add the spinach. Stir well and
  cook until wilted.

- Adjust the seasoning to taste and cool to one side.

- Heat the vegetable oil in a large heavy-based saucepan to 180°C / 350F.

- Wet the rim of the wrappers with water and fold into a triangle, then form a cone
  around your fingers, sealing one edge, but keeping the case open.

- Fill with the vegetable curry before sealing well, wetting the rim again
  if necessary.

- Deep-fry, in batches of 4, for 4–5 minutes; flip the samosas halfway
  through cooking.

- Drain on kitchen paper as you deep-fry the remaining samosas.

- Serve the samosas warm with pots of the yoghurt raita for dipping.

TOP TIP

- If you can't find samosa wrappers, spring roll wrappers make a good alternative.

Pani Puri

Serves: 4   Preparation time: 30–35 minutes   Cooking time: 12–15 minutes

INGREDIENTS

110 g / 4 oz / ⅔ cup dates, pitted

1 tsp tamarind paste

a pinch of ground ginger

½ tsp caster (superfine) sugar

½ lime, juiced

salt and freshly ground black pepper

a large bunch of mint, leaves picked

1 ½ tbsp distilled vinegar

350 g / 12 oz / 1 ½ cups plain yoghurt

400 g / 14 oz / 2 cups canned chickpeas
    (garbanzo beans), drained

100 g / 3 ½ oz / 1 cup paneer, cubed

a small bunch of coriander (cilantro),
    finely chopped

450 g / 1 lb / 3 cups wholewheat flour

1 tbsp sunflower oil, plus extra for oiling

1.25 l / 2 pints 4 fl. oz / 5 cups vegetable oil,
    for deep-frying

METHOD

- Combine the dates, tamarind, ginger and a pinch of sugar in a small saucepan.

- Stir well, then add 75 ml / 3 fl. oz / ⅓ cup of water; bring to a simmer and cook until the dates are soft.

- Blitz the mixture in a food processor, then season to taste using lime juice, salt and pepper.

- Cover and chill until ready to serve.

- Blitz together most of the mint leaves with the vinegar and a little water in a food processor until paste-like in consistency. Season to taste before transferring to a bowl and covering.

- Chop the remaining mint leaves and stir them into the yoghurt in a small serving bowl. Season to taste, then cover and chill.

- Combine the chickpeas, paneer, coriander and seasoning in a small mixing bowl. Season to taste before covering and setting to one side.

- Sieve the flour into a large mixing bowl with 1 tsp of salt, then add the sunflower oil and enough water to make a firm dough.

- Turn out the dough and knead very briefly before dividing into 12 pieces.

- Heat the vegetable oil in a large, heavy-based saucepan to 180°C / 350F.

- Oil your hands before rolling the pieces of dough into balls.

- Roll out the balls into rounds approximately 7 cm (3 in) in diameter.

- Deep-fry the puris, one by one in the hot oil, until puffed and golden, pressing them down with the back of a slotted spoon to help them cook evenly.

- Drain on kitchen paper and repeat for the remaining puris.

- Serve the cooked puris with the chickpea salad, raita and chutneys for dipping.

TOP TIP

- Traditionally, the puris are loaded with the accompaniments and eaten whole, so don't roll them out too wide!

Gulab Jamun

Serves: 4   Preparation time: 2 hours 20 minutes   Cooking time: 10–12 minutes

INGREDIENTS

6 cardamom pods, crushed with seeds removed

2 cloves

375 g / 13 oz / 1 ½ cups caster
    (superfine) sugar

300 ml / 10 ½ fl. oz / 1 ¼ cups water

1 tsp rose water

150 g / 5 oz / 1 cup dried milk powder

55 g / 2 oz / ⅓ cup plain (all-purpose) flour

½ tsp baking powder

a pinch of salt

1 tbsp whole milk

1 tbsp melted ghee or sunflower oil, plus extra
    for oiling

1.25 l / 2 pints 4 fl. oz / 5 cups vegetable oil,
    for deep-frying

METHOD

- Grind the cardamom seeds and cloves until powdery, then add to the sugar and water in a saucepan.

- Heat over a medium heat until the sugar has dissolved, then increase the heat and bring the syrup to a boil for 2–3 minutes until thickened.

- Remove the syrup from the heat and stir in the rose water, then strain through a sieve into a clean jug.

- Cover and set to one side.

- Combine the milk powder, flour, baking powder and salt in a large mixing bowl.

- Mix in the milk and ghee until a dough starts to form. Mix in a little more milk if it's too dry, taking care not to overmix.

- Pinch off small balls of the dough and roll between oiled palms into balls, then arrange on a tray and cover with a towel.

- Heat the vegetable oil in a large, heavy-based saucepan to 180°C / 350F.

- Deep-fry 4–5 of the balls of dough at a time until golden brown all over. Remove with a slotted spoon and place in a baking dish.

- Pour over the prepared syrup and leave the gulab jamun to soak for 2 hours before serving.

TOP TIP

- A squeeze of fresh lime juice over the top will cut through the sweetness of this traditional dessert.

Yakitori

Serves: **6**   Preparation time: **15 minutes**   Cooking time: **8–10 minutes**

INGREDIENTS

2 tbsp honey

55 ml / 2 fl. oz / ¼ cup mirin

75 ml / 3 fl. oz / ⅓ cup sake

75 ml / 3 fl. oz / ⅓ cup light soy sauce

2 large chicken breasts, diced evenly

4 large closed cup mushrooms, sliced

2 tbsp groundnut oil

salt and freshly ground black pepper

250 g / 9 oz / 2 cups cooked short-grain rice

METHOD

- Preheat the barbecue or grill to a moderately hot temperature and soak some wooden skewers in cold water for 30 minutes.

- Whisk together the honey, mirin, sake and soy sauce with 2 tbsp of water in a small saucepan.

- Bring to a simmer over a medium heat, stirring to help dissolve the honey. Continue to cook until reduced and thickened slightly.

- Thread the diced chicken onto the skewers before brushing with the prepared marinade.

- Thread the sliced mushrooms onto skewers before brushing with groundnut oil and seasoning with salt and pepper.

- Grill the chicken yakitori for 8–10 minutes, turning occasionally, until the meat is cooked through and golden all over; the mushrooms skewers will only take 4–5 minutes.

- Serve the yakitori and mushrooms over bowls of rice.

TOP TIP

- The chicken can be substituted for diced duck breast or cubes of rump/sirloin steak, as well as seafood such as peeled prawns or scallops.

Prawn Gyoza

Makes: 16   Preparation time: 25–30 minutes   Cooking time: 10–12 minutes

INGREDIENTS

2 tbsp groundnut oil

3 cm (1 in) piece of root ginger, peeled
    and minced

2 cloves of garlic, minced

2 spring onions (scallions), finely chopped

450 g / 1 lb / 3 cups raw prawns (shrimp),
    peeled, de-veined and chopped

2 tbsp mirin

2 tbsp rice wine vinegar

1 tbsp dark soy sauce

a pinch of chilli (chili) flakes

16 10 cm (4 in) gyoza wrappers

55 ml / 2 fl. oz / ¼ cup sesame oil

dark soy sauce, to serve

METHOD

- Heat the groundnut oil in a large wok or sauté pan set over a moderate heat until hot.

- Sauté the ginger, garlic and spring onions for 2–3 minutes, stirring frequently, then add the chopped prawns.

- Cook the prawns for 2 minutes, then add the mirin, vinegar, soy sauce and chilli flakes.

- Reduce the heat and cook for a further 2–3 minutes, stirring occasionally, then remove from the heat.

- Once the filling has cooled slightly, take a gyoza wrapper in the palm and fingers of one hand and spoon a generous teaspoon of the filling into the centre.

- Using your fingertip, wet the rim with a little water before sealing the gyoza, using a pinching method to create a crimp.

- Repeat this process until all the gyoza have been prepared.

- Place a large frying or sauté pan over a moderate heat until hot. Arrange half of the gyoza in the pan and add 100 ml / 3 ½ fl. oz / ½ cup of water.

- Cover the pan with a lid and steam for 2–3 minutes. Remove the gyoza from the pan and dry on kitchen paper, then add the remaining gyoza and repeat the steaming process.

- Once all the gyoza have been steamed, add 2 tbsp of sesame oil to a dry frying pan set over a moderate heat until hot.

- Pan-fry the gyoza in batches, using fresh oil between batches, until golden brown.

- Serve with soy sauce for dipping.

TOP TIP

- For a vegetarian take, use chopped Portobello mushrooms for the filling instead of the prawns.

Pad Thai

Serves: 4   Preparation time: 10–15 minutes   Cooking time: 11–14 minutes

INGREDIENTS

2 tbsp fish sauce

3 tbsp rice wine vinegar

2 tbsp cold water

1 lime, juiced

1 tbsp dark soy sauce

1 tbsp dark brown soft sugar

3 tbsp groundnut oil

salt and freshly ground black pepper

350 g / 12 oz / 2 ⅓ cups raw prawns (shrimp),
    peeled and de-veined

2 cloves of garlic, minced

2 large eggs, beaten

350 g / 12 oz / 3 cups cooked rice noodles

75 g / 3 oz / 2 cups beansprouts

2 tbsp peanuts, crushed

1 tbsp chilli (chili) sauce

2 shallots, finely sliced

a small bunch of coriander (cilantro),
    leaves picked

METHOD

- Whisk together the fish sauce, vinegar, water, lime juice, soy sauce and sugar in a small mixing bowl until the sugar dissolves.

- Heat 2 tbsp of the oil in a large wok or sauté pan set over a moderate heat until hot.

- Season the prawns, then stir-fry for 2–3 minutes until pink and tender. Remove to a plate and reduce the heat under the wok.

- Add the remaining oil along with garlic, sautéing for 1 minute.

- Add the beaten egg and cook until scrambled, then add the noodles, beansprouts, 1 tbsp of peanuts and the prepared sauce.

- Toss everything together and cook for 4–5 minutes, tossing frequently, until the noodles are glossy and the sauce has reduced.

- Stir the prawns into the noodles along with the chilli sauce and warm through for a few minutes.

- Season to taste, then lift into bowls and serve with the remaining peanuts and shallots and coriander leaves on top.

TOP TIP

- Diced turkey breast works well in this dish; finish with a sprinkling of crushed peanuts.

Papaya Salad

Serves: 4   Preparation time: 1 hour 10 minutes   Cooking time: 8–10 minutes

INGREDIENTS

75 ml / 3 fl. oz / ⅓ cup groundnut oil

1 tbsp rice wine vinegar

1 tbsp lime juice

1 tbsp fish sauce

1 tbsp light soy sauce

2 cloves of garlic, minced

1 red chilli (chili), deseeded and finely chopped

1 tbsp soft light brown sugar

salt and freshly ground pepper

2 large skinless chicken breasts, thinly sliced

165 g / 5 ½ oz / 1 ½ cups green (string) beans, trimmed

2 papayas, peeled and thinly sliced

3 tbsp peanuts, lightly crushed

METHOD

- Prepare a quick dressing by whisking together 55 ml / 2 fl. oz / ¼ cup of the oil with the rice wine vinegar, lime juice, fish sauce, soy sauce, garlic, chilli and sugar until the sugar has dissolved.

- Heat the remaining oil in a large wok or sauté pan set over a moderate heat until hot.

- Season the chicken and sauté for 6–7 minutes until golden and cooked through.

- Remove to a plate and leave to cool slightly, then cover and chill for up to 1 hour until cold.

- Once the chicken is cold, cook the beans in a large saucepan of salted, boiling water for 2–3 minutes until al dente. Drain and toss with a little of the prepared dressing.

- Arrange the beans on plates and top with the papaya and the cooked chicken.

- Spoon over more of the dressing and garnish with peanuts before serving.

TOP TIP

- Julienned, firm mango flesh would make a delicious substitution for the papaya in this salad.

Bibimbap

Serves: 4   Preparation time: 15 minutes   Cooking time: 20 minutes

INGREDIENTS

110 g / 4 oz / 1 cup thin rice noodles

2 tbsp sesame oil

2 tbsp groundnut oil

2 cloves of garlic, minced

400 g / 14 oz / 2 ⅔ cups beef mince

3 tbsp light soy sauce

½ tsp soft light brown sugar

2 spring onions (scallions), thinly sliced

1 red chilli (chili), thinly sliced

400 g / 14 oz / 3 ½ cups cooked white rice

2 Portobello mushrooms, outer skin peeled
    and sliced

100 g / 3 ½ oz / ½ cup enoki mushrooms

½ small red cabbage, shredded

110 g / 4 oz / 4 cups beansprouts

2 large carrots, peeled and sliced into thin
    matchsticks

2 orange peppers, deseeded and thinly sliced

2 heads of pak choi, leaves separated and
    thinly sliced

4 medium eggs

2 tbsp red chilli (chili) paste

METHOD

- Cook the rice noodles in a large saucepan of boiling water for 3–4 minutes until tender. Drain and toss with the sesame oil to prevent sticking.

- Heat the groundnut oil in a large sauté pan set over a moderate heat until hot.

- Add the garlic and sauté for 1 minute before adding the beef mince.

- Cook until the mince has browned all over, then add 2 tbsp of soy sauce and the sugar.

- Stir well before spooning into a bowl, then mix the remaining soy sauce with the spring onions and chilli and set to one side.

- Add the rice to the pan and warm through over a moderate heat before spooning into heatproof bowls.

- Top with the beef and arrange the vegetables and noodles on top in separate piles.

- Preheat the grill to a hot temperature.

- Carefully crack an egg on top of the vegetables and flash under the grill until the white and yolk are just set.

- Remove from the grill and serve immediately with the spring onions and chilli in soy sauce and chilli paste on the side.

TOP TIP

- Why not try using pork or chicken mince instead of beef next time you make bibimbap?

Pho

Serves: 4   Preparation time: 10 minutes   Cooking time: 20–25 minutes

INGREDIENTS

2 tbsp groundnut oil

4 cloves of garlic, crushed

5 cm (2 in) piece of root ginger, peeled
    and chopped

2 star anise

1 tsp black peppercorns

½ tsp coriander seeds

2 lemongrass stalks, crushed

1.5 l / 2 pints 4 fl. oz / 6 cups vegetable
    or chicken stock

225 g / 8 oz / 2 cups ribbon rice noodles

400 g / 14 oz / 2 ⅔ cups raw prawns (shrimp),
    peeled and de-veined

2 tbsp fish sauce

1 tbsp rice wine vinegar

1 tbsp soft light brown sugar

1–2 tbsp light soy sauce

2 shallots, thinly sliced

4 spring onions (scallions), sliced diagonally

a small bunch of coriander (cilantro),
    roughly chopped

3–4 red chillies (chilies), finely sliced

METHOD

- Heat the oil in a large saucepan set over a moderate heat until hot.
- Add the garlic, ginger, star anise, peppercorns, coriander seeds and lemongrass and fry for 1 minute until aromatic.
- Add the stock and stir well before bringing to the boil.
- Reduce to a simmer and cook gently for 10 minutes, then strain the broth into a clean saucepan.
- Return the broth to a simmer before adding the noodles; let them simmer in the broth for 6–8 minutes until tender.
- Add the prawns and let them cook for 4–5 minutes until pink and tender.
- Season the pho with fish sauce, rice wine vinegar, sugar and soy sauce to taste.
- Ladle into bowls and garnish with shallots, spring onions, coriander and chilli on top before serving.

TOP TIP

- Substitute half of the broth for coconut milk for a creamy, decadent version of this fragrant soup.

Bahn Mi

Makes: **2 large sandwiches**   Preparation time: **25 minutes**   Cooking time: **20 minutes**

INGREDIENTS

110 ml / 4 fl. oz / ½ cup water

55 g / 2 oz / ¼ cup golden caster
   (superfine) sugar

55 ml / 2 fl. oz / ¼ cup distilled vinegar

1 tbsp fish sauce

450 g / 1 lb piece of pork loin, trimmed

salt and freshly ground black pepper

1 cucumber

1 large carrot, peeled and cut into thin batons

1 large white onion, thinly sliced

2 green chillies (chilies), sliced

3 tbsp groundnut or sunflower oil

1 large French baguette

a large bunch of coriander (cilantro), torn

1 tbsp chilli (chili) oil, to serve

METHOD

- Combine the water, sugar, vinegar and fish sauce in a saucepan. Whisk over a moderate heat until the sugar has dissolved.

- Bring the liquid to the boil, then reduce to a simmer for 10 minutes. Remove from the heat and leave to cool to one side.

- Line a chopping board with a couple of sheets of cling film, then place the pork loin on top and flatten out with a meat tenderiser.

- Slice the pork loin into strips and season generously with salt and pepper.

- Roughly peel the cucumber and slice into long, diagonal slices.

- Toss the cucumber, carrot, onion and chilli in the prepared dressing. Leave to sit as you cook the pork.

- Heat some of the oil in a large sauté pan or wok set over a high heat until hot.

- Stir-fry the pork in batches for 3–4 minutes until golden. Remove the cooked pork to a plate and use a little fresh oil to fry each batch.

- Remove the ends of the baguette before cutting it in half; split each half horizontally before opening them up.

- Arrange some of the dressed vegetables and chilli in the baguettes, then top with pork.

- Garnish with coriander and a little chilli oil if desired before serving.

TOP TIP

- Substitute the green chillies (chilies) for sliced green peppers to cool down this classic Vietnamese sandwich.

Fried Sesame Cake

Serves: 4   Preparation time: 1 hour 25–30 minutes   Cooking time: 6–8 minutes

INGREDIENTS

600 ml / 1 pint 2 fl. oz / 2 ½ cups warm water

225 g / 8 oz / 1 cup caster (superfine) sugar

2 tbsp baking powder

450 g / 1 lb / 3 cups glutinous rice flour

250 g / 9 oz / 1 ⅔ cups rice flour

250 g / 9 oz / 1 cup sweetened red bean paste

200 g / 7 oz / 1 1/3 cups white sesame seeds

1.5 l / 2 pints 12 fl. oz / 6 cups vegetable oil, for deep-frying

METHOD

- Whisk together the water and sugar in a large mixing bowl until the sugar has dissolved.

- Add the baking powder and stir well until dissolved.

- Add the flours and stir well until a soft dough has formed; it should be a wet clay consistency, so add a little more water if too dry.

- Pinch off golf-ball-sized pieces of dough and flatten into rounds using the palm of your hands.

- Spoon a few tablespoons of the red bean paste onto the rounds, then bring the edges up and around the filling and seal well.

- Roll the sealed dough between your palms to help shape it into round balls.

- Roll the balls in the sesame seeds to coat, then arrange on a lined tray and leave to rest, covered loosely, for 1 hour.

- After an hour, heat the vegetable oil in a large, heavy-based saucepan to 160°C / 325F.

- Fry the sesame balls, in batches, for 3–4 minutes until golden brown all over.

- Drain on kitchen paper and cook the remaining cakes before serving warm.

TOP TIP

- Try rolling the balls in black sesame seeds for a visual contrast.

Jerk chicken

A popular choice

AMERICAS

Mississippi mud pie

Food on the move

Pulled Pork Bun

Serves: 4   Preparation time: 15–20 minutes   Cooking time: 1–1 ¼ hours

INGREDIENTS

2 tbsp sunflower oil

1 onion, finely chopped

3 cloves of garlic, minced

salt and freshly ground black pepper

1 tsp ground cumin

a pinch of ground cinnamon

a pinch of Cayenne pepper

100 ml / 3 ½ fl. oz / ½ cup tomato ketchup

100 ml / 3 ½ fl. oz / ½ cup cider vinegar

2 tbsp soft dark brown sugar

450 ml / 16 fl. oz / 2 cups chicken stock

800 g / 1 lb 12 oz piece of pork shoulder, trimmed and scored

125 g / 4 ½ oz / ½ cup barbecue sauce

4 sesame seed buns, split

75 g / 3 oz / ½ cup gherkins in vinegar, drained and sliced

METHOD

- Heat the oil in a large casserole dish set over a moderate heat until hot.
- Add the onion, garlic and some seasoning and sweat until golden.
- Add the ground spices, stir well and cook for a further minute, then add the ketchup, vinegar, sugar and chicken stock.
- Bring to a simmer, stirring well, before adding the pork and covering. Cook at a steady simmer for 1–1 ¼ hours until the pork is tender, then remove from the sauce and pat dry.
- Shred the pork before stirring back into the sauce; season to taste.
- Preheat the grill to hot and toast the sesame buns until lightly golden.
- Top the bottom halves with pulled pork and a little barbecue sauce.
- Garnish with chopped gherkins and sit the bun tops in place, then serve.

TOP TIP

- Fresh sliced avocado adds a creamy texture to these sandwiches.

Gumbo

Serves: **4** Preparation time: **15 minutes** Cooking time: **35 minutes**

INGREDIENTS

3 tbsp sunflower oil

1 onion, finely chopped

2 sticks of celery, finely chopped

1 green pepper, deseeded and finely chopped

2 cloves garlic, minced

2 tsp ground cumin

2 tsp ground coriander

2 tsp paprika

a pinch of Cayenne pepper

a pinch of caster (superfine) sugar

salt and freshly ground black pepper

350 g / 12 oz / 3 cups okra, tops removed

3 plum tomatoes, deseeded and chopped

250 ml / 9 fl. oz / 1 cup water

400 ml / 14 fl. oz / 1 ¾ cups coconut milk

METHOD

- Heat the sunflower oil in a large casserole dish set over a medium heat until hot.
- Sweat the onion, celery, pepper and garlic for 6–7 minutes, stirring occasionally until they start to soften.
- Add the ground spices, sugar and some seasoning to the vegetables and stir well.
- Cook for a further minute, stirring occasionally, then stir in the whole okra and chopped tomatoes.
- Cover with the water and coconut milk, stir and bring to a simmer.
- Simmer for 20–25 minutes until the okra are soft and tender.
- Adjust the seasoning to taste before serving in bowls.

TOP TIP

- Add a couple of sliced chorizo sausages to the gumbo for a real Louisiana treat.

Shrimp Po'boy

Serves: 4   Preparation time: 15 minutes   Cooking time: 4–6 minutes

INGREDIENTS

1 tbsp paprika

1 tbsp garlic powder

2 tsp onion powder

2 tsp dried thyme

2 tsp dried oregano

½ tsp caster (superfine) sugar

salt and freshly ground black pepper

450 g / 1 lb / 3 cups raw prawns (shrimp), peeled and de-veined

3 tbsp sunflower oil

1 tbsp lemon juice

110 g / 4 oz / ½ cup plain yoghurt

110 g / 4 oz / ½ cup mayonnaise

a pinch of Cayenne pepper

a large white baguette or sub roll, split

2 large vine tomatoes, sliced

a large handful of rocket (arugula)

METHOD

• Preheat the grill to a moderately hot temperature.

• Stir together the ground spices and herbs (except the Cayenne pepper), sugar and 1 tsp each of salt and pepper in a large mixing bowl.

• Add the prawns and toss well to coat in the spice mixture.

• Heat the oil in a large frying pan set over a moderate heat until hot.

• Fry the prawns, in batches if necessary, for 2–3 minutes until they turn pink and are tender to the touch.

• Transfer the prawns to a warm plate and season with lemon juice.

• Whisk together the yoghurt, mayonnaise, Cayenne and seasoning in a small bowl.

• Lightly toast the cut side of the bread for 1 minute, then remove from the grill and spread the bottom half with the yoghurt and mayonnaise sauce.

• Top with slices of tomato and some rocket, then arrange the prawns on top.

• Sit the top of the toasted bread over the prawns before serving.

TOP TIP

• Fried oysters would make a classic filling for a po'boy sandwich.

Philly Cheesesteak

Makes: **2 large cheesesteaks**   Preparation time: **10 minutes**   Cooking time: **15–20 minutes**

INGREDIENTS

3 tbsp sunflower oil

2 tbsp unsalted butter

2 large onions, sliced

salt and freshly ground black pepper

2 green peppers, deseeded and sliced

450 g / 1 lb / 1 ½ cups bavette or rump steak, trimmed and thinly sliced

2 large sub rolls or demi baguettes, split

8 slices of hamburger cheese or provolone

METHOD

- Heat together 2 tbsp of oil and 1 tbsp of butter in a large sauté pan set over a moderate heat until hot.
- Sauté the onions with salt and pepper for 5–6 minutes until softened and starting to brown.
- Reduce the heat and add the peppers, then continue to cook for another 3–4 minutes until caramelised.
- Remove the vegetables from the pan and wipe it clean.
- Add the remaining oil and butter and increase the heat under the pan to high.
- Season the slices of steak and fry in the oil and butter for 3–4 minutes until just cooked through.
- Return the vegetables to the pan to warm through; season to taste.
- Preheat the grill to hot.
- Line the rolls with slices of cheese and top with the steak and vegetables.
- Flash the cheesesteaks under the grill for 1 minute, then remove and serve.

TOP TIP

- Sliced, pickled green jalapeno peppers would add a welcome vinegary kick to these cheesesteaks.

Key Lime Pie

Serves: 8   Preparation time: 4 hours 20 minutes   Cooking time: 24–28 minutes

INGREDIENTS

5 limes, juiced and zest grated

225 g / 8 oz / 1 ½ cups digestive biscuits, crushed

125 g / 4 ½ oz / ½ cup butter, melted

2 large egg yolks

2 tbsp icing (confectioners') sugar

400 g / 14 oz / 2 cups condensed milk

2 large egg whites

a pinch of salt

100 g / 3 ½ oz / ½ cup caster (superfine) sugar

½ tsp cream of tartar

METHOD

- Preheat the oven to 160°C (140°C fan) / 325F / gas 3.
- Juice and zest 4 of the limes; slice the remaining lime and reserve as a garnish.
- Combine the crushed biscuits and melted butter in a large mixing bowl until they resemble wet sand.
- Press the mixture into the base and sides of a 18 cm (7 in) fluted, springform tart tin and use the back of a tablespoon to help create an even finish.
- Bake for 10 minutes, then remove to a wire rack to cool.
- Beat the egg yolks and icing sugar in a large mixing bowl with an electric whisk, then add the condensed milk and beat thoroughly for 2–3 minutes until thick.
- Add the lime juice and zest and beat again for 2–3 minutes, then pour into the tin on top of the baked base.
- Increase the oven to 190°C (170°C fan) / 375F / gas 5.
- Whisk the egg whites with a pinch of salt in a large, clean bowl until softly peaked.
- Gradually whisk in the sugar and cream of tartar until stiff and glossy.
- Spread the meringue over the lime filling and spread it out across the pie.
- Bake for 14–18 minutes until golden brown on top.
- Remove to a wire rack to cool before chilling for 4 hours until cold.
- Turn out the pie and garnish with slices of lime before serving.

TOP TIP

- Try using different citrus fruits for the filing such as grapefruit or orange.

Mississippi Mud Pie

Serves: 8   Preparation time: 20–25 minutes   Cooking time: 30–35 minutes

INGREDIENTS

250 g / 9 oz / 1 ⅔ cups bourbon biscuits, crushed

75 g / 3 oz / ⅓ cup unsalted butter, melted

200 g / 7 oz / 1 ⅓ cups dark chocolate, chopped

175 g / 6 oz / ¾ cup butter, cubed

4 large eggs, lightly beaten

165 g / 5 ½ oz / 1 cup soft dark brown sugar

3 tbsp cocoa powder

250 ml / 9 fl. oz / 1 cup double (heavy) cream

1 tbsp icing (confectioners') sugar, for dusting

METHOD

- Preheat the oven to 160°C (140°C fan) / 325F / gas 3.

- Combine the crushed biscuits and melted butter in a mixing bowl. Press two-thirds into the base and sides of a 18 cm (7 in) straight-sided, springform cake tin, then chill for 10 minutes.

- Melt the chocolate and butter in a heatproof bowl set over a half-filled saucepan of simmering water and stir occasionally until smooth.

- Meanwhile, beat together the eggs and brown sugar in a large mixing bowl until pale and thick, then add the cocoa powder and whisk again briefly.

- Fold the cream and melted chocolate mixture into the eggs and sugar. Once thoroughly incorporated, pour the mixture onto the biscuit base.

- Top with the remaining biscuit mixture, spreading it out evenly before baking for 30–35 minutes.

- Remove to a wire rack and leave to cool completely.

- Once cool, turn out and dust with icing sugar before serving.

TOP TIP

- Try baking mini marshmallows into the centre of this pie to create a vibrant look.

Poutine

Serves: 4   Preparation time: 15–20 minutes   Cooking time: 6–8 minutes

INGREDIENTS

1.25 l / 2 pints 4 fl. oz / 5 cups vegetable oil,
   for deep-frying

1 tbsp cornflour (cornstarch)

1 tbsp water

3 tbsp unsalted butter

2 tbsp plain (all-purpose) flour

325 ml / 13 fl. oz / 1 ⅓ cups beef stock

salt and freshly ground black pepper

450 g / 1 lb / 4 cups frozen French fries

150 g / 5 oz / 1 ½ cups Cheddar cheese curds

METHOD

- Heat the oil in a large, heavy-based saucepan to 180°C / 350F.

- Whisk together the cornflour and water in a small bowl, then set to one side.

- Melt the butter in a small saucepan set over a medium heat until hot.

- Once the butter has melted, whisk in the flour and cook until dark golden and smooth, then gradually whisk in the beef stock until you have a slightly thickened gravy.

- Bring to the boil before reducing to a simmer. Thicken as necessary by whisking in the cornflour mixture.

- Season to taste and keep over a very low heat as you cook the fries.

- Deep-fry the fries, in batches, for 3–4 minutes until golden and crisp.

- Drain the fries on kitchen paper and place in a mixing bowl. Season with salt, then add the cheese curds and a little gravy.

- Toss well to coat before arranging in a bowl; top with more gravy before serving.

TOP TIP

- If Cheddar cheese curds are not available, chopped mozzarella makes a good substitute.

Rice and Peas

Serves: 4   Preparation time: 20 minutes   Cooking time: 15–20 minutes

INGREDIENTS

2 tbsp vegetable oil

1 green pepper, deseeded and finely diced

½ tsp dried thyme

150 ml / 5 fl. oz / ⅔ cup long-grain white rice, rinsed in warm water for 15 minutes then drained

400 ml / 14 fl. oz / 1 ¾ cups chicken stock

200 g / 7 oz / 1 cup canned kidney beans, drained

100 g / 3 ½ oz / 1 cup frozen peas, thawed

salt and freshly ground black pepper

hot sauce, to serve

METHOD

- Heat the oil in a large saucepan set over a moderate heat until hot.

- Add the pepper and thyme and sauté for 3–4 minutes, then stir in the drained rice.

- Stir the rice well to mix in the oil and peppers, then cover with the stock.

- Bring to the boil before reducing to a gentle simmer, stirring in the kidney beans.

- Cover with a lid and cook gently for 15–20 minutes until the rice has absorbed the stock.

- Remove the rice from the heat and add the peas on top of the rice before covering with a lid again; leave for 10 minutes.

- After 10 minutes, fluff the rice with a fork and season to taste. Serve with hot sauce.

TOP TIP

- Try swapping the red kidney beans for butter beans and a large handful of fresh peas.

Jerk Chicken

Serves: 4   Preparation time: 1 hour 20 minutes   Cooking time: 35–45 minutes

INGREDIENTS

75 ml / 3 fl. oz / ⅓ cup vegetable oil

1 Scotch Bonnet chilli (chili), deseeded

1 tbsp paprika

a pinch of Cayenne pepper

1 tsp dried thyme

½ tsp ground allspice

2 tbsp hot sauce

1 tbsp light soy sauce

1 tbsp caster (superfine) sugar

salt and freshly ground black pepper

1 lime, juiced

2 tbsp water

4 chicken legs, trimmed and cleaned

2 red onions, roughly chopped

2 courgettes (zucchinis), roughly chopped

2 yellow peppers, deseeded and chopped

1 red pepper, deseeded and chopped

METHOD

- Whisk together half of the oil with the chilli, ground spices, sauces, sugar and seasoning.

- Make a few slashes in the skin of the chicken, then rub the marinade into the chicken. Cover and chill in the fridge for 30 minutes.

- Remove the chicken from the fridge and leave to stand at room temperature for 30 minutes as you preheat your grill to a moderately hot temperature.

- Once the chicken has come up to room temperature, place under the grill and cook for 35–45 minutes, turning a few times, until the meat is cooked through; the thickest part of the legs should read at least 74°C / 165F on an instant-read thermometer.

- Remove the chicken from the grill and leave to rest, covered loosely with aluminium foil.

- Toss the vegetables with the remaining oil and plenty of seasoning, then grill for 8–10 minutes until tender and lightly charred.

- Serve alongside the chicken.

TOP TIP

- Cooking this dish on the barbecue works really well and adds a great smoky taste.

Goat Curry

Serves: **4**   Preparation time: **30 minutes**   Cooking time: **1 hour 15–20 minutes**

INGREDIENTS

55 ml / 2 fl. oz / ¼ cup vegetable oil

salt and freshly ground black pepper

750 g / 1 lb 10 oz / 5 cups diced goat shoulder, trimmed

2 onions, chopped

3 cloves of garlic

5 cm (2 in) piece of root ginger, peeled and minced

3 red chillies (chilies), sliced

2 tbsp mild curry powder

1 tsp dried thyme

a pinch of Cayenne pepper

400 g / 14 oz / 2 cups passata

400 ml / 14 fl. oz / 2 cups coconut milk

250 ml / 9 fl. oz / 1 cup lamb stock

½ white or hispi cabbage, roughly chopped

METHOD

- Heat 2 tbsp of oil in a large casserole dish set over a moderate heat until hot.

- Season the goat, then seal in batches, adding more oil if necessary, until golden all over. Remove to a plate.

- Reduce the heat under the dish before adding the onion, garlic, ginger and chilli. Sweat for 6–7 minutes until lightly browned.

- Add the spices and stir well before covering with the passata, coconut milk and stock, then bring to the boil.

- Reduce to a simmer and return the goat to the dish, then cook gently for 1–1 ¼ hours until the goat is tender.

- Add the cabbage to the dish and braise for 10–12 minutes until softened.

- Adjust the seasoning to taste and serve.

TOP TIP

- Goat meat can be hard to come by; mutton makes a perfectly acceptable substitute in this curry.

Beef Tacos

Serves: 4   Preparation time: 20–25 minutes   Cooking time: 15–20 minutes

INGREDIENTS

3 tbsp sunflower oil

1 large green pepper, deseeded and finely diced

1 large red pepper, deseeded and finely diced

1 onion, finely chopped

3 cloves of garlic, minced

1 tbsp ground cumin

2 tsp smoked paprika

½ tsp dried thyme

½ tsp dried oregano

a pinch of caster (superfine) sugar

500 g / 1 lb 2 oz / 3 ⅓ cups lean steak mince

200 g / 7 oz / 1 cup canned chopped tomatoes

125 ml / 4 ½ fl. oz / ½ cup beef stock

2 large ripe avocados, pitted and chopped

½ red onion, finely chopped

1 lime, juiced

a dash of hot sauce

salt and freshly ground black pepper

4 large corn taco shells

METHOD

- Heat the sunflower oil in a large casserole dish set over a moderate heat until hot.

- Add the peppers and the onion. Sauté for 5–6 minutes, until lightly browned, then add two-thirds of the garlic.

- Add the spices and sugar; stir well and cook for a minute, then add the steak mince.

- Brown the meat well, then stir in the chopped tomatoes and beef stock.

- Bring the mixture to a simmer, then reduce the heat and cook for 15–20 minutes.

- Season to taste before leaving to cool slightly.

- Mash together the avocado, red onion, lime juice, hot sauce and the rest of the garlic until smooth; season to taste.

- Spoon the beef into the taco shells, then serve with the guacamole on the side.

TOP TIP

- A spoonful of queso fresco or crumbled feta cheese will lend a pleasing tang to these tacos.

Pulled Pork Burritos

Serves: 4   Preparation time: 20–25 minutes   Cooking time: 35–40 minutes

INGREDIENTS

2 tbsp sunflower oil

1 large onion, finely chopped

2 cloves of garlic

450 g / 1 lb piece of pork tenderloin, diced

1 tbsp tomato purée

1 tbsp dark brown soft sugar

150 g / 5 oz / ⅔ cup barbecue sauce

350 ml / 12 fl. oz / 1 ½ cups warm water

salt and freshly ground black pepper

4 large flour tortillas

2 large ripe avocados, pitted and chopped

1 lime, juiced

a dash of hot sauce

½ iceberg lettuce, shredded

4 vine tomatoes, cored, deseeded and
    finely chopped

75 g / 3 oz / ¾ cup Monterey Jack, shredded

METHOD

- Heat the oil in a large casserole dish set over a moderate heat until hot.

- Add the onion and garlic and sauté for 3–4 minutes until golden.

- Add the pork and continue to cook for a few minutes until lightly browned, then stir in the tomato purée and sugar.

- Cover with the barbecue sauce and water and bring to a simmer, stirring well, then cook at a gentle simmer for 35–40 minutes until the pork is very tender.

- Once the pork is ready, shred it using a couple of forks and season to taste.

- Mash the avocado with lime juice, hot sauce and seasoning to taste.

- Lay the tortillas on a flat surface and spread with some guacamole, then top with shredded lettuce and some tomato.

- Top with the pork and some cheese before rolling and serving.

TOP TIP

- Canned refried beans can be warmed and used as a filling in these burritos.

Quesadillas

Serves: 4   Preparation time: **20 minutes**   Cooking time: **6–10 minutes**

INGREDIENTS

2 tbsp olive oil

300 g / 10 ½ oz / 2 cups spicy sausages
    (chorizo, kabanos etc.), skin removed

150 g / 5 oz / 1 ½ cups Cheddar or
    Monterey Jack, grated

a small bunch of coriander (cilantro), chopped

2 red peppers, deseeded and sliced

4 large flour tortillas

salt and freshly ground black pepper

METHOD

- Preheat the grill to a moderately hot temperature.

- Grill the sausages for 6–8 minutes, turning occasionally, until golden and sizzling, then remove to a plate lined with kitchen paper.

- Cut the sausages in half and flatten using the back of a spatula or fish slice.

- Arrange the cheese, coriander and peppers over 2 of the tortillas, drizzle with olive oil and season with salt and pepper.

- Sit the sausages on top before laying a tortilla over the fillings.

- Lift the filled tortillas onto a grilling tray; toast under the grill, one at a time, for 2–3 minutes, then flip and cook the other side for another 1–2 minutes until golden brown.

- Remove from the grill and cut into portions before serving.

TOP TIP

- Whisk together two thirds yoghurt to one third mayonnaise; season and serve as a dip on the side.

Seafood Tostadas

Serves: 4   Preparation time: 15 minutes   Cooking time: 15 minutes

INGREDIENTS

2 tbsp olive oil

450 g / 1 lb fresh tuna

salt and freshly ground black pepper

4 large vine tomatoes, cored, deseeded
    and chopped

a small bunch of coriander (cilantro), some leaves
    picked and some chopped

55 g / 2 oz / ½ cup white Cheddar, grated

2 limes, cut into wedges

a dash of hot sauce

8 small soft flour tortillas

METHOD

• Preheat the grill to a moderately hot temperature.

• Brush the tuna with the olive oil and season with salt and pepper.

• Grill for 8–10 minutes, turning once, until cooked through and firm to the touch,
  then remove from the grill and leave to cool slightly.

• Once cool enough to handle, flake the tuna into a mixing bowl using a fork.

• Add the tomatoes, chopped coriander and cheese and stir well.

• Squeeze in a little lime juice and hot sauce and season to taste.

• Warm the tortillas under the grill, then fill with the tuna.

• Garnish with coriander leaves and serve with the remaining lime wedges.

TOP TIP

• Mahi mahi or sea bass would make a delicious alternative to the tuna in
  these tostadas.

Empanadas

Serves: 4   Preparation time: 25–30 minutes   Cooking time: 25–30 minutes

INGREDIENTS

2 tbsp olive oil

150 g / 5 oz / 2 cups chestnut mushrooms, sliced

salt and freshly ground black pepper

100 g / 3 ½ oz / ⅔ cup prosciutto, sliced

100 g / 3 ½ oz / 1 cup mozzarella, sliced

½ tsp dried oregano

½ tsp dried basil

350 g / 12 oz ready-made shortcrust pastry

a little plain (all-purpose) flour, for dusting

METHOD

- Heat the olive oil in a large frying pan set over a moderate heat.
- Sauté the mushrooms with a little salt and pepper until they are golden brown.
- Drain on kitchen paper, then mix in a bowl with the prosciutto, mozzarella, dried herbs and a little more seasoning.
- Preheat the oven to 180°C (160°C fan) / 350F / gas 4 and line a large baking tray with greaseproof paper.
- Roll the pastry out on a lightly floured surface to 5 mm (¼ in) thickness.
- Cut out four 18 cm (7 in) rounds of pastry and spoon the filling into their centres.
- Wet the rim of the pastry with a little water using your fingertip, then fold the bottom end over the filling and crimp with the opposite side to seal.
- Transfer to the baking tray and bake for 25–30 minutes until the pastry is golden and cooked.
- Remove from the oven and leave to cool a little before serving.

TOP TIP

- For vegetarian empanadas, swap the prosciutto for some cooked, cubed white potato.

INDEX

Picture Credits

4–5 enviromantic / Getty Images, 11 (bl) Kevin Clogstoun / Getty Images, 38 (br) Dennis K. Johnson / Getty Images, 39 (bl) Tim Gerard Barker / Getty Images, 38–39 (main) Gary Yeowell / Getty Images, 62–63 (main) Steve Allen / Getty Images, 63 (bl) Craig Ferguson / Getty Images, 94 (br) Andrew Burton / Getty Images, 95 (bl) Angus Oborn / Getty Images, 94–95 (main) Ed Norton / Getty Images

1, 3, 6–7, 8, 10–11 (main, cl), 62 (br) © Thinkstock / Getty Images

Food photography and recipe development: PhotoCuisine UK